I LOVE CATS

by. Harold T. Rober

LERNER PUBLICATIONS ◆ MINNEAPOLIS

Note to Educators:

Throughout this book, you'll find critical thinking questions. These can be used to engage young readers in thinking critically about the topic and in using the text and photos to do so.

Lerner Publications Company
A division of Lerner Publishing Group, Inc.
241 First Avenue North
Minneapolis, MN 55401 USA

For reading levels and more information, look up this title at www.lernerbooks.com.

Library of Congress Cataloging-in-Publication Data

Names: Rober, Harold T., author.
Title: I love cats / by Harold T. Rober.
Description: Minneapolis : Lerner Publications, [2017] | Series: Bumba books—Pets are the best | Audience: Ages 4–8. | Audience: K to grade 3. | Includes bibliographical references and index.
Identifiers: LCCN 2015043847 (print) | LCCN 2015045327 (ebook) | ISBN 9781512414134 (lb : alk. paper) | ISBN 9781512415179 (pb : alk. paper) | ISBN 9781512415186 (eb pdf)
Subjects: LCSH: Cats—Juvenile literature.
Classification: LCC SF445.7 .R58 2017 (print) | LCC SF445.7 (ebook) | DDC 636.8—dc23
LC record available at http://lccn.loc.gov/2015043847

Manufactured in the United States of America
1 – VP – 7/15/16

Expand learning beyond the printed book. Download free, complementary educational resources for this book from our website, www.lernerresource.com.

Table of **Contents**

Pet Cats

Cats make great pets.

There are many kinds
of cats.

Our cat has long hair.

We brush our cat often.

Brushing keeps cat hair clean and smooth.

Cats like to scratch.

They have sharp claws.

Our cat uses a scratching post.

Why do you think cats use scratching posts?

Playing is fun!

Cats play with toys.

They jump high and

run fast.

Most pet cats stay inside.

Sometimes our cat goes outside.

We put a leash on our pet.

Why should you put a leash on your cat?

Cats eat cat food.
They drink fresh
water too.
We feed our cat two
times each day.

We train our cat to use a litter box.

We take turns cleaning it.

Why do we train cats to use a litter box?

Our cat goes to the veterinarian.

A veterinarian is a pet doctor.

She makes sure our cat is healthy.

Cats can live for

many years.

We take good care of

our pet cat!

Cat Supplies

scratching post

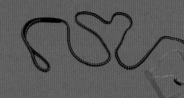

leash

litter box

brush

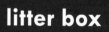

food dish

toys

water dish

Picture Glossary

leash

a strap used to hold and control a pet

litter box

a box pet cats go to the bathroom in

scratching post

a special post for pet cats to scratch

veterinarian

a doctor who is trained to treat sick or hurt animals

Index

Read More

Brannon, Cecelia H. *Pet Cats.* New York: Enslow Publishing, 2017.

Fortuna, Lois. *Caring for a Pet.* New York: Gareth Stevens Publishing, 2016.

Heos, Bridget. *Do You Really Want a Cat?* Mankato, MN: Amicus, 2014.

Photo Credits